CASTAWAY

by

Yvette Christiansë

DUKE UNIVERSITY PRESS

Durham and London

1999

Publishing Acknowledgments:

"And When I Write, the Muscles in My Chest Move" in
The Breaking Line, Youngstreet Poets, vol. 5.

"Desire" in *Southerly Magazine,* autumn 1995; *Columbia Magazine,*
no. 24/25; *The Breaking Line,* Youngstreet Poets, vol. 5.

"Eclipse" in *Barrow Street,* vol. 1, no. 1, November 1998.

"For the Arrival of a Serious Enemy" in *West Coast Line,* fall 1996.

"For the Record" in *Southerly Magazine,* autumn 1996.

"Geography Lesson" in *Southerly Magazine,* autumn 1996.

"Letter to General D'Albuquerque—On the Pleasures of Taste" in
Midday Horison—First Choice of Australian Poets, Round
Table Publications, 1996; *Southerly Magazine,* autumn 1996.

"One More Mile, One More Town" in *West Coast Line,* fall 1996.

"She Confesses" in *Southerly Magazine,* autumn 1996.

"The Cabin Girl Sings of Love, Reluctantly and into an Empty
Sky" in *The Breaking Line,* Youngstreet Poets, vol. 5.

"The Island Sings Its Name" in *Southerly Magazine,* autumn 1996.

"The Sleeper" in *West Coast Line,* fall 1996.

"The Voyage Out" in *Barrow Street,* vol. 1, no. 1, November 1998.

Designed by Amy Ruth Buchanan
Typeset in Monotype Garamond by Tseng Information Systems, Inc.
Library of Congress Cataloging-in-Publication Data appear on
the last printed page of this book.
This book was completed with the support of a Project
Development Grant from the Literature Board of the Australia
Council.

Nobody is only of themselves or
the moment they inhabit

This book is dedicated to the loving memory of
Margaret Delphine Blandford
and honors
Sally Veronica Blandford Christiansë
William Bennett Blandford
Lynette Shern Christiansë
Jean-Pierre Christiansë
and,
with especial love and gratitude,
Roz Morris

Contents

The Name of the Island

in memoriam
Marguerite Delphine Ritch Blandford
b. 1898? St. Helena–d. 1974 Sydney

My grandmother's island is
wrapped in its own ocean and a fog
that whispers and sings to itself
since lighthouses and watermarked maps
put reefs out of business and
exiles no longer smoulder into their diaries
in the gloom of rock and rain.

Napoleon, when he was grinding his teeth
in the bleak mists of his last stand—
growing fat and miserable, cut off
from his old standard-bearers and the
static of muskets crackling through the hills
of Badajoz where the stench made horses
rear and foot soldiers sag at the knees—
Napoleon named it the worst place.

⋆

All night the ocean squabbled
along the foreshore. The long house
creaked and went tighter, tighter
like a corset around a sick man's liver.

None of the doctors would listen.
He told them, he could feel it growing,
as if he had a child there, and him
a man amongst men. Giving birth now
to his own sick liver

while the ocean threw salt
up onto the rocks and the wind
and sand and whipped the house

like a father whipping a child
that howled and howled
under the anchor of his hand.

✦

Standing at the window
when the wind scours the rockface
for the smallest remnant of brightness,
Bonaparte-now-Buonoparte is as good as
married to the losses that twitter and nibble
all around him, that come up the drive
clogging the spokes of carriage wheels,
flake from his thinning hair when he
drags his fingers through it.

The tragedy of existence: that a man can never
see the top of his own head or the back of his own
head, or the side of his face. Not really. Ever. While
others can see things. If he has a speck of dust on his
cheek, a flake of ash on his hair, a small bare spot
bare enough for a gob of well-aimed spit.

✦

Good neighbours, like good mirrors and good family.
And good family like a house, square and firm
facing the right sun, the right wind.

Napoleon Bonaparte-not-Buonoparte if you please,
wishes for a good house facing the right sun.
And his mother. And says his name over and
over as if it is a limb he must massage or
lose to the butcher's field knife.

✦

Suddenly, the rock grates, screeches
like a gull dashing down
from a full dark sky
and the man sits up, up

out of its sharp reach
up, up out of the dream
of something falling horribly
into the field surgeon's pail.

Now the wind brings them.
Green as sickness, they gather
on the other side of his window,
gather and stretch far back, right
down to the dock, and out onto the water,
like ants that have found a honey trail.

They gather like silence for a man
woken horribly without another
to turn to. And the wind is whistling
an old marching tune through the mane
of a stiff dead horse.

No more the ride like a god
through the troops, no more
the grand gilt pose on the rampant
white stallion. Only the wind and the rock
and the army of faces, faces,
green faces like sickness.

                    ✦

One day it strikes him, how the wind blows
through the rock and the house, and the rock
and the house are like thinning, graying hair
on a sick man's head. Another day, the wind
is a bushel of rats, bristling in his hat. He
rummages in his hat now before raising it to the light.

Still another day, the wind pierces the
walls of the house, the walls of his body,
like a finger pushing into his intestines.
He can point exactly where the intrusion
took place. He wants it marked, where, one night

he woke from a dream of an Englishman
thrusting a finger into his diaphragm
and separating his organs.

Most days, the wind
is just the wind and the island
does not even support nightmares.

The Island Sings Its Name

My grandmother's voice is
wrapped in distance and tissue papers
rustling like the leaves
of a favourite tree
in the first cool signs of Autumn,
a proof that things will turn
and even the most loved

will be taken away, leaf by leaf
until mornings have other voices
given you by new people and new places
that can take so much and
only so much of things
they have never seen
and cannot even spell.

✦

Writing your name, having never
written it before—never? in over thirty years,
years that take in a first day at school,
love, anger, your last day?—
I stumble over an "e" or "r"
and don't know how your mother
would have written you, or if it was
your father—the man who married again—who
wrote your name. The first time.

✦

And now my mother tells me
1898. "We think." And the date
sheers the edge off things,
cuts through rock and digs itself
into the ground and I'm diving
in, after it to catch it, hold it
by its high-tempered tail
in the hope of hitting pay dirt—

the glint beyond cinnabar or fool's gold,
like dreams of running down streets
or calling up at windows or
into the mist that brews
like pre-dawn tea held
in a working man's hands. I want
the real thing. The
way you smiled. And I want
you to smile at me, as if
you are . . . always.

✦

Like a tree they'd circle
with a ring of stones,
with a bronze plaque to say
you've outlived monarchs
and their proclamations, the
rise of borders and the fall
of roly-poly men and their roly-poly chests,
the rustle around the world
as young men nuzzle their cheeks
into the blue-black hips
of their slender barrels of steel,
the litany of elegies flickering briefly
in living-rooms between one bracket
of Ads and another, one mouthfull
and another.

✦

I want
to be small enough
to slip into the bough of your arm
to hear your spine creak
in the moonlight, when the house
slumps heavy on its foundations
and all is as well as a circle
of elders who replenish themselves
like waves in a slate-green ocean
that can take the worst news.

I want
to be sure there is more
than watching you shrink
suddenly, then slowly. Then
vanish.

And you who gave me first words — the
language for clocks and names for lorries
and rain and manners like
how to say please and thank you —
you took all words away,
lying there so straight and small and calm.

.✦.

And being a girl from an island
long ago in her blood
and far away from being
cast off from all sides
as she was, those last days,
she wished for the sea.

Like the wind caught indoors
and held underfoot
on hot days, she longed
for the sea. Not any sea,
but that green sea
she knew hurled down
past the mud-plastered flats
of Lorenço Marques where the paraffin woman
charged a family this many escudoes
for one night under a rain-filled canvas;
the white beaches
of the wedding-cake hotel.

Longing, as persistently
as the wind at a door, a loose key hole,
the old leaden kind, and door latch
made for the ball of a thumb.
Whispered in the night

about Lorenço Marques
and drove her sweltering granddaughters
mad. And the sweltering granddaughters
balling their fists against their ears
in their high and dry landlocked youth
blew far off course on this, not knowing
why it was the sea
that set foot on the salt-gray jetties
of old Lorenço Marques
that she longed for, the sea she
could set her foot on like a lady
stepping into a longboat
on the side of a barnacled old hull
she is glad to see the stern of.

Marguerite Delphine, but never called,
except with "Finnie." Fin. For the
fin of a sleek dark fish
that finds a current and slips
clean into its long sweep
all the way around the world
without moving a muscle. A
flurry of colour shooting out
at the slicing edge of the bow.
The wings of birds that fly
in that other, heavy sky
that also holds a moon and
smashes a sun into trillions.

Finnie. For Delphine. Something
her mother liked.
Head-and-shoulders above the rest,
to bear her down the road, set on
school books. If school books came.
But. No school books.

They named her
second side of the road,
back door black,

hands in the washtub. They
named her pointed at
and slinking shadow. When
all she was was
her mother's girl.

And All Things Come to Pass

One night, close to the equator:
seeing ten stars fall. And the crew
shuddering in their sleep. The hull
trembling like an animal left out
in the cold. And these stars—I carry
them in my head still—have nothing
to do with me. One fell close—its fierce
whispering quarrel with the water
as it cast its name like knives in every
direction. The ash and steam of its name.
The water that fought it, pulled and opened
an irresistible mouth. That burning entry
of the once light of all things.

On Being Restless

Tonight, I feel them stir
rise and swerve, these flocks—
taken up flight in the
blind hours, out here where
the steady wash cleanses
our cutting hull—

not desires for hands or those
prayers for pleasure,
more pleasure, but the
other tugging—when a scent
rises from the air and defies
the anchorage of a name, an

explanation. The depth of a
sky as it reaches above flat-
bottomed clouds that boat
out of the longitudes
where islands recite their
green rosaries. The long

cry of a wintering bird,
pulling the air to itself,
like a shawl or hospital blanket,
or, simply another voice.
Yes, these things,
I feel them stir

and rise and swerve
as if I am walking through
their nesting ground. I watch the
dark, not seeing a thing except my
own moon's shadow, but I hear
their wings make light of night.

Letter to General D'Albuquerque—
On the Pleasures of Taste

J'avais, j'avais ce goût de vivre loin des hommes,
et voici que les Pluies (St.-John Perse, *Pluies*)

Last night when the rains came like tongues
on the lances of a devil god—the one I saw
that night your mast pricked the horizon,
made a hole big enough for you to enter
with your pincers and tongs, your burning
coals and mission of The Book—I sat up
like a lost man, the lost man I have become—
for the man who loses his tongue and at least
one hand, not to mention a nose and ears is,
you would agree, lost even in the eyes of
those who may have known him. Last night

when the rains came like tongues on the
lances of a devil god, I reached for water.
Such thirst. And do you know, General,
how hard it is to quench a thirst when you
have no tongue? A tongue, I have discovered—
O great conqueror and true believer—is
necessary for many things. Ask the man who
savours an evening meal as he rides the last
miles home, or the woman who trembles as she
holds her lover's tongue in her mouth, or the
child who holds its ground with one rude gesture.

I would taste the salt on the air as it blows
from that graveyard, the ocean I once loved. I
would taste the rain and learn to tell where
it has risen from and what year, like a
connoisseur of wines, and I would be drunk
too soon for refusing to spit an atom away.

Once, once I had a taste for living far from men, but now the rains (St.-John Perse, *Rains*)

I would learn every story and song from every
leaf, even those that blow in like tired birds
on their migrations around the world. I would
break open lemon after lemon in my lemon groves
and douse my missing sense, oh what is my stolen

sense, and dance to the agony of that delight,
General. I would be able to tell you chapter
and verse of every book in The Book you held up
to my face in your anger. Do you know, great
hero and measure of the world, I have learnt
that words must be like fruit—each a taste,
each an ingredient for a palate in need of
refreshment: "ocean," an orange from Tangier
as its peel breaks away from the pale soft
pap it wears—and I have always loved the
pith of citrus, for its temperament; "mouth,"

an apple from any orchard, but one that's lain
long in a storeroom and gathered its sweetness
like a bride and groom in the weeks before
they are allowed to touch—ah, their smiles
at the banquet. I could offer you more, like
morsels for a guest at my table, this table of
rock and a mountain that grows other mountains
like a strange tree dropping strange fruit. I
would find a way to tell their vintage, their
good years and poor and always wash my mouth
clean with the simple taste of water, dear General.

Fernão Lopez traveled to Goa in the early 1500s with Afonso D'Albuquerque, Por-
tuguese general and coloniser of the region, who left him in charge of a group of
Portuguese to settle and "rule" the local population. On his return, D'Albuquerque
found that Lopez and others had converted to Islam and sided with Moslem resis-
tance to the Portuguese. Upon capture, Lopez and other "renegades" were punished
by having their right hands and the thumb of their left hands severed. Their tongues,
ears, and noses were also cut off as a reminder of their treachery. Lopez's hair and
beard were scraped off with clam shells in a process known as "scaling the fish." He
remained in India for some years until he was to be returned to Portugal. He left
his ship at the then uninhabited island of St. Helena, becoming its first exile and a
figure of curiosity and myth. He planted lemon groves and tended a flock of goats.
There are claims that Defoe based Robinson Crusoe on Lopez.

Letter to General D'Albuquerque —
On the Pleasures of Touch

Vieil homme aux mains nues
(St.-John Perse, *Images a Crusoe*)

Now it is especially wicked, now it is grandly
cruel—the goats bring their muzzles to me
each morning, as if to have them tested.
And perhaps there are things I know nothing of,
things that go on in the island's sharp dark,
things that threaten their downy chins
while I sleep with my arms around myself.
Perhaps it is those things I must reassure
them against. So they come, nuzzling like
children, sweet children. And, oh my General—
you man amongst men—I am like a woman
who mourns the loss of her breasts.

It is the memory, sire, the memory that is
cruel, crueler than the coal-singed axe,
the cauterising blade, crueler than pain
that hammers itself into bronze bracelets
around a man's wrist, or into the heart
of the wife he will never see again.
I tell you, the roughest surface,
the coarse pink of a tiger's tongue—
I would calibrate each ridge, each edge
and take the marks they leave as
their signals of love and affection for
what is now my missing joy, General, oh

voyager of the spicy world, soldier
of steel, maker of punishments our God
would admire. Memory is the worst thing

Old man with naked hands (St.-John Perse, *Image for Crusoe*)

in the morning and in the fluid night—
those times of waking and entering sleep.
In some places, those places you know
nothing of—except as places that
fill your scales and our King's hands—
oh hands, hands that end in the flurry
of fingers rifling through the wind, the
hair of a favourite child, a laughing woman's
skirts, fingers that search for knots in a beard,

pluck melodies from halls in a different heaven
like fruit from the leaves of the generous tree—
in those places—and there are sounds
you will never dream of—those places
where a man can forget the body of Christ
to savour instead the delight of dancing
on the back of a blue boy-god who licks
butter from his fingers—in those places
there are rituals to mark the arrival of night,
its retreat. They secure the heart's many gates,
ease all passages, and memories are sweetened
around their saddest edges, General.

But. Here. Surviving the inquisition of
nights in the island's heretical winds.
Without the simplest protection for
the palm of my hand, or against the flea
that can only be pinched loose by quick fingers—
oh, what is missing is the intimacy
between forefinger and the soft ball
of the thumb. My General, defender of the
Faith, great man and angel of the seas,
the morning visit of my goats breaks my heart.
And there are days I long to invite you to
breakfast, here amongst the muzzles of innocence.

Letter to General D'Albuquerque—On Desire

Grain. The yellow scent a cool quiet mat
under her bare feet. I kissed everything
that day. And I curse you, General. Hell
and more hell to you. Nails under your feet.
Heat in the most delicate tissue of your bowel.
I kissed the leaves of trees too dumb
in their drunken green to know. I kissed
the leavened bread. I kissed the holy shadow
of the gate over a celibate's path.

And it was never enough. Not if
there were twice as many blades
of grass. And I kissed the moon-glazed
water gathering on the tiles where
rain fell—that air of heaven itself
breaking to its knees. And there was
no god but her, no paradise or judgment
but her. And what do you kiss when you are
on your own, Caesar of the East? What hands
remind your skin? Is there a woman who comes
and does she sing over your body, raise it
to where the waters will not even hold a bird?

And do you forget borders and destinations,
duties and the long reigning lies of countries
and their citizens? Do you kiss her for the
sounds in her throat? Do you kiss her for
the length of her fingers and the tips of her
hair? Do you kiss her for the lance of desire
that lays you low at the gates of your body?
Do you pray with the art of a bird singing
as you are transformed and take off into
those avenues of the wind that carry you
in her smooth wake above crazy storms
and tortured trees? I ask you this, General
as one whom you have taught about distance and desire.

Letter to General D'Albuquerque — On Solitude

On other days the island breaks its anchorage,
begins a strange migration from gravity's wide domain,
begins to separate as if dust from dust itself,
as if all this rock has been the illusion
which we, and I in particular, have served
for some steady purpose that travels
with us wherever we go, in full health or
in every range and degree of sickness.

On such days, Oh Great Reader of the Winds
and Hand at the Helm, the light that accompanies
the disintegration is the light of tiny insects
disturbed by memory and forgetfulness
as the island separates and lifts in silence,
and there is no-one to turn to, to ask,
"Is this real?" On such days, I press the
palm of my hand to my mouth, find in the
palm of my hand all anchorage, all gravity

and the measure of distance — say, the sun from
this unstable place, the tip of a leaf to its stem,
the interval between the print of my left foot
and the print of my right — all distances in
the palm of my hand, even this sacrilege itself,
General. And who is here to chastise my false
astronomy, my diabolical upheaval of God's
universe? My goats shift together on these days,
not a satanic hair between them, careful of their throats.

And I range the full length of where, on other days,
most days, the island keeps its normal hours,
holds its normal shape. Look to the east and
that is me, to the west and I am the same while
the island rests still and golden in the space of

angels. I write of this to you, my General, protector
of my faith. Write back soon, send word
if you are eager to join me. I will show you
how to close your ears to the noise of angels
as they walk about the island before they send it back.

Letter to General D'Albuquerque — On Forgiveness

Ha! qu'on m'évente tout ce leurre!
(St.-John Perse, *Vents*)

When I was a boy and even, yes, as a man,
I took pleasure in pollens that made soldiers sneeze.
I knew the arrival of girls who had walked through
flower beds by the notes that swirled around them —
those portions of air which have been dusted by stamens
and sing of these quick touching interludes, General,
the private pleasures and excitements hidden from all
but for the sun glinting on their eyelashes, the quick
delicate dip and flare of their nostrils. And I have
loved the air around horses fresh from a morning canter,
the flanks of the rider who strides up newly washed stairs
past vases of day-old roses bred from the Malagasy strain.

But oh, I must tell you, General, most measurable man,
I must tell how those soft messages of air that charm
and delight in other places — those places I have lost
and those you have conquered — those delights are
a different matter here. They cut and sting, and
some days I burn as if in hell. And I long for the
silence of pollen-free days. The pallor of empty
air. And some days I lower myself to remorse
like a man who has lost his head for arrogance
before God. Some days I ask if there are
things that cannot be forgiven, and what
the worst punishment would be. Some days

I believe it is to be lost entirely, to
slip through the cracks that appear after
the island has shaken itself in rage
against its anchorage, out here, between
the whalers and cargo ships, the man-o-wars

Ha! let all this delusion be aired out! (St.-John Perse, *Winds*)

and sailors who cough and spit in the
acrid mornings. Ah, but then . . . that talc
stirs, the spores of rebellion rise, and
I welcome the buckshot that blows from the
smallest blossom, so small a spider may crush it.
On these days, my General of Generals,
Governor of our King's good fortune, I approach

something that is close to forgiveness.
I forgive the yellow flower whose name
I do not know. I forgive it for the innocence
of its face. I forgive the sweet bearded goats
for the exhalation of their coarse hides
which shed stiff gray hairs into the milk
I claim from them. And have you drunk
their milk, oh Caesar of the spicy seas?
Have you tasted its earth, and has your
head turned, grown tight around the temples,
and are you reminded as I am of the grave
in which we will lie, waiting for the trumpet's call?

For the Devout Mouth

One Amen. To keep the palate clear of blasphemies.

The yellow melon's flesh is without sin.
And the word that is delightful to God
is fit and right as nectar nurtured in the flesh
of a bird just clean of its plumage.

Then let us lay our hands flat on the wood
and praise fire for where there is no wood
there is no rest in the thrall of a storyteller
fresh from a good feast delivered by the Lord.

And let us keep our tongues soft, not to deserve
the marrow of bones left last on our plates, but to
praise the seed of apples which *are*
like prayers of gold in pictures of silver.

Let us eat so much as is sufficient though our lips
shine with honey. Let us reserve a portion of hunger
and curse the vomit of the belly made heavy
by the flattery of a mouth swimming with a poor man's gold.

Let us keep our hems low in defiance of evacuation
and those fires of the innermost corners of the belly.
Let us find perfumes and ointments in the throats
of flowers that fall across our table and sweeten our breath.

Let us defy the fig tree, the falling plum,
the pomegranate and orange whose insides
leak onto our fingers and stain our sleeves.
Let us hide under the covers of thirst and hunger.

Let us spell out p-r-u-d-e-n-c-e
in the far country of temptation.
Let us remember that dogs go low and

serpents lower in servitude to their bellies.

Let us cure ourselves of this island

before we anoint our right hands,
betray ourselves with the ghosts
who haunt the fringes of leaves
and steal all sense, even the limits of our shadows.

For the Record

He called for his scribe.
Like that . . . whatsisname? The old
monarch English children sing of?

He called for his scribe, not pipe. No
bowl. Unless a full-stemmed red
newly-delivered from Corsica. And
no fiddlers, only the scribblers
writing with one eye on history—
ah, they touch his shadow
just to know their names will be
mentioned, at least, by historians
and even idle browsers, years, perhaps
centuries, from now. So.

Before his own past and present are lost
to the liars and those silly women in tidal pools
of skirts and ribbons, he called for Emmanuel
August Dieudonne Marius Joseph de Las Casas,
that man so like a bird, eyes sharp for
the bluest gems for history's mantle.
Not the Sevres bowls or snuff boxes
cosseted in the hull of a ship slipping
into the beggaring winds, then heaved
by beasts onto this land of the damned.

Ah. These few things. An empire in
a bowl, in a snuff box—and how the
devil had been in his sneezes as they
shook the world to its miserable core.
Las Casas, scratching away to keep up,
was after nothing smaller than the
Italian Campaign and those . . . others.
But good. Because—he touched his head,
shivered—before you know it,
it's vanished. Or ceased to matter.

Like—that morning his foot touched
French soil—not booted and stepping off
the boat, but the morning he stood barefoot . . .
Gone. Only a sense. Like the perfume of a woman
he'd made love to in . . . Ah. That too.
Or that day when . . . How much effort,
pushing at something that is blocked,
pulling at a tiny thread that gives
nothing, not much of the grand things,
not at this moment. And when he was a boy.

But. It is the women that are a worry. How
many, how many times? Had he really
trembled for just one? Had she really
made his hand slide loose
from a letter, the stem of a glass,
fumble nervously at his hair. No one
on this island to dazzle or be dazzled by.
Only a girl with enough pepper in her
to make the fallen sneeze with delight.
But then, as truth may show

not so much women as countries
had he desired. Victory. All those
dainty little principalities . . . still
tasting them as sweat on his upper lip.
Ah yes. The tinkle of a cavalryman's
accouterment, the creak of a saddle
as he cranes to see higher than his
vantage over the infantrymen. These . . .
enticing little niceties. These
occupy the private seconds of . . .

All this confounded idleness! Planting
tomatoes? Like that lost soul
he's heard some mention of—Lopez,
was it? One hand, no nose, no ears
or tongue. Living on this howling . . .
this rock of the damned for decades,
alone but for goats, a cockerel

and a single species of bird.
Planting things, like an Adam.
Well, he's no Adam. Planting

things to take the edge off
waiting for death. *We are all*
waiting to die. Everything we do is
something to do until we die. We
are here to die. Born to die.
I'd die for an orange from Tangiers,
for a kiss, a glimpse, a night . . .
Ah. But he knew about death. Don't
put that into the great history. How he'd
known the art of sowing deadwood across Europe.

But this island . . . God! This . . .
nowhere. Nowhere? Sending someone
of his stature to nowhere. Swines.
The world is made up of swines, bitches,
goats and floating turds. And then
someone who sees above it grabs out
and they heave to their oxen toes
and send him to nowhere. Uh, how
exhausting. This place makes everything
exhausting. And if only the wind would

stop. For a day. One blessed day to have
free ears again. That is the horror of this
nowhere, that his ears are subjected
to this incessant torture. The
most effective revenge of swines.
He is without ears — hearing nothing
but the wind screeching over Deadwood Plane
or dragging out the cries from
passing slave ships and mothers of boys
laid deep in the furrows of old campaigns.

So. What shall he dictate — to counter
the diarists' scribble, to distract himself
from the rude wind? What they expect,

of course. Reassessments? Not what they
hope for. Schemes. Something for a new
monetary system? What do they have now
instead of napoleons? A new legal code?
How do they disorganise themselves now
around the shambles of their continent?
Perhaps a new philosophy for exploring blame.

So. What to set down? Aah. If only. The
scent of dew sweetening the blades of grass
around his tent as his generals stand
in the lamplight, their shadows swaying
into the travel-yellowed muslin like
serpents from India. His heart had never
beaten like this. It beats now as if it must,
or lose the last chance to move like a love-
startled heart, a chance that passes in this place
where time and his body conspire with the wind.

Sleigh Ride

He's never heard so much noise. Not even
in battle — that time at Badajoz when
the stench hung in the pall for days
and birds stuttered through the murk
as he made his escape. All this noise.

He cursed the ocean, its
name that bristled with long, bladed
currents ready to swoop down the globe
as he'd dreamt of swooping across
Europe, maybe even into Asia. The noise

surrounded the long-house, became
its outer walls like a snow
of sorts, a covering that forced
its own silence out of him. In
the midst of the hungry noise which

held the sound of his sleigh —
that dry rushing sound which cut
a way through the snow of that
cursable land, that reduction of
dreams, that place of black snow — even

the heartbeats of women sitting
in the church pews of Leipzig while
canons startled the Minister's sermon
and carriage wheels chased after hooves.
All surrounded his swine of a house now

in the full path of the ocean's venom,
day into night into weeks. Would he
live? Could he live in this . . . weathering
of his heart, his spirit? Was this, then,
purgatory? Alone in a house

full of whispering people, people whose nibs
scratched away like rats nibbling
or scuttering into a bag of grain.
Keeping their journals, they are.
Every word he said, or a gesture

they'd cornered out of the rest. Alone
with the constant record of his life —
the present made up in others' scribbling,
the past flung up on the swine rocks
and recited by the slate-green ocean

without end. O, that rushing sleigh
cutting out of the ice and snow,
the long line of his army reaching
back as far as he had reached forward.
Had there been that many men in the world?

One night . . . the sleigh bumping. He thought
over bodies as he woke, but the sleigh
rushed on and now it was here carrying
him again, in a nightmare
that would never end in quiet, since
he is learning, having stood at the window
and seen nothing but the stillness of death
laid out by the jaundiced moon, that
the ocean's restless spleen is a mere rustle
against the vortex rushing within.

The Enemies of Progress

Did he ever tire of battlefields?
This one, yes. This enemy.
Not the English bag of piss and
bloat sweltering under the buckles
of his title. Governor. *Pff!* But
that mercenary in his camp.

Ruthless. Rattling at the windows
like a thousand gun carriages
dragging in the blood, wounds and
death. Hissing like a snake
in the hot belly of a
wild man from India.

If only he could find a rebel
strand among the scythes.
Hell. How many men had fallen
exactly where they stood?
O hell. Dead on the ground.
Count. Send for the count. No,

to hell with that. Find more.
There. Reeling east, the brilliant XIVth.
Secure that ridge. The musket fire
making the sky creak like an
old leather saddle. And who
was dragged in the stirrup

beside his horse? Who laid down
in the red sheets and turned
his head like a swan at dusk?
Who came carried through
three times dealt with in the
leg, hiding his face in his helmet?

Bring up the reserves I tell you.
Now. Are those the screams of
fighting men, or dying men? Here,
you. You, with the hand that
waves but never moves. Quick,
which camp blows that bugle?

And no. No walk through the
sunset fields. The glow of
the horizon hides one thing,
shows another. The pride is
smothered in evening. Damn
sunsets on the battlefield.

Necessary Things

A brief dream in the mouth of all this
noise: he was flogging the ocean
like a guardsman flogging his doxy

for raising her skirts in the shadow of
his absence. It cried out like a
woman, tried to run. He held it back,

beat it with his salt-stung whip,
the sweetness of the welts it left. The
size of his erection as she raised

her skirts, rolled over and raised her
rump. The glimpse of that violent place,
a saint's battered lily folding

with guarded pleasure long before
he entered, his breath hissing
in his ears and in his throat the

language of foot soldiers guffawing
over cards and rum as they waited
their turns. For months, he hoped for

the dream's return, till he felt it
suck him into a place he had never been.
A place of suspended plans. So he practiced

a pragmatic defense only
the washerwoman knew as she laid
his sheets out to the bleaching wind.

The Emperor Considers the Fate of His Book

Kirchenhoffer? Kirchenhoffer? Yes
another slippery turnabout, another
successful transmogrification from slime-
going slouse. A man steeped in the ancient,
counting ciphers on the rims of his
nails, counting hairs on the legs of
flies and finding royal tombs in every
corporal's eyes. So, Kirchenhoffer
gives to the world a fallen Emperor's secret
passion. Kirchenhoffer joins
the ranks of silly women plaiting
unfortunate fantasies into their
skewering fingers as they plan
husbands and squalling offspring.
Hooferkirch, krich-n-huffer sitting
there in a wasted freedom, selling
to the world—ah, the English,
the English buying, they think,
Fate, the future. Fools

> *The Book of Fate, formerly in the possession of
> and used by Napoleon, rendered into the English language
> by H. Kirchenhoffer from a German translation of an
> ancient Egyptian manuscript found in the year 1801, by
> M. Sonnini in one of the royal tombs near Mount Libycus
> in Upper Egypt*

is a fraud
unless you are Fate itself,
unless you are born this way.
And Kirchenhoffer is a slime-
bellied panhandler of puny proportion.

Last Battles

How? Growling down into the gravel
of a rough dream that dragged the
lids off coffins, he stopped
at the grave of Osimandeus. Or
was it Alexander? Yes, Alexander.
But the single howling question . . .

shaking the quiet lichen from its
settling place. He stood before the end
once more, saw the last hope die and him,
not given to poetry or nonsense, wanting
to sing a lament a troubadour may have sung
to a lady far from butchery and defeat.

A Very Sick Man

Trying to describe it. Already an entity
that has possessed him, it swells.

In the dome of his diaphragm—an
unholy incense, the Devil's Mass
in progress in his body. Reduced
and remembering. Once, as a boy,
his mother entering his fever . . .

room. The sound of her progress
across the floor boards. A good
sound and his heart had filled.
There is—is there?—a happiness
that must come as when hearing

young angels sing. Something like that.
But behind her, the room. Corners
scowling under their waiting hoods.
Those waiting corners. And now
in this corner of the swinish globe,

the hoods sway in the aisles of his body,
dismembering the caduceus of health,
inverting it for their sour incense.
And his liver, the censor they swing
at the high altar of his mind.

And he fears his own raving.
Orders himself . . .
No raving . . . as
the thin green halo glows
around his hands.

One More Mile, One More Town

On the Friday they swarmed through.
A man said "like Cossacks through a village."
Blades wamped air and if they caught
insects, no one knew. Neither did
the bar girls care, who counted each
wamp a stroke that would earn
crisp notes while their skin wilted
and clung to their flesh like
cotton sheets in the sweating
afternoon. Men who owned sheets
sat in the stuttering corners
under fans that stirred the
body-lodged air and it was hard
to tell what they were really like,
if they thought through the ceiling
that shuffled and creaked
while the boys will be boys
ploughed and slid along the
narrow ruts of their night-
mares. The woman who sat
one day with her legs apart
as if too hot—she was the one
who turned her head and sighed,
long ago shifted to the side,
and what was left in the place
she had emptied were her eyes.
A man said "Eyes like a bloody
cunt" and the boys being boys
shivered under their fresh sweat
as one so that the farm boy saw
the butcher's window, the softness,
the thickness and the city boy saw
the sheep caught by the mud at the edge
of the dam—"It's the dry, it went in
for the water, got caught by the
soft stuff," someone said, swatting.

Face to Face

Here they come. Ridiculous. Riding up
as if they are going to a zoo. Fresh from
China, or India. As if they haven't seen
enough. As if they can never be satisfied.

Well. Here they come. To see a man they
warn their children with. He snorts,
disappears into the small room. Wishes for
high walls as he'd never wished for borders.

What he would like is to stare at them,
see what China has done, or India,
to their faces. He has a growing theory
about places. Places have more power

than armies. Places, he believes now,
march into a face, into the tiny, unattended
pores in one's skin and erect themselves
as markers, signs, sometimes even as

illness. He wants to see China and
India. Or the miserable outposts
under siege to blood-sucking insects,
carnivores that snarl behind

darkness and put an end to sleep.
Places rife with the limbs of coolies,
Guineamen, Hindus, housemaids and
water boys, nose-ringed vendors,

people who swallow fire and dance
with snakes, who can take blades
into their stomachs, skewers into
their eyelids to the applause of

the marketplace. He wants to see
how the burrs and mud of such places

attach themselves to a passing
skirt, a shabraque. He wants to see

fleas breeding on a lap dog's back,
and foraying out into wider fields
for that soft, pink foreign flesh;
birds that circle with wide black

shadows. He wants to see how these
places conquer the stupid faces that
leave their ships and struggle up this
rock to peer across the Governor's

ditches in the hope of seeing a bogeyman.
He wants to see the invasions. Perhaps
there are tracks where a place has raced
and skidded, wheeled about and taken stand

in the hollow of a cheek, under an eye.
Perhaps there are signs of alliances
between wind, sun and stone to force
the softness to the surface. Perhaps

he could see the haematic glow of a
hot damp place, its hosts of moving
things in the jowls, the corners of
the eyes, the way a handkerchief is

raised to daub an upper lip. He wants
to see how the sheer spectacle of
a place, the encounter alone — spiced
by legends before one face, fanned by

the distance behind one's back —
corrodes that inexhaustible supply of
middle-ranked livers. He wants to see
this on their faces when they stare.

Brotherhood

If, as he now knows, a face is
overtaken, say, by a place, if as he
feels, a face begins to wear the effects
of a place as anyone—highest or low—

may wear a garment for an occasion—
and here the occasion being his
occupancy of this less-than-miserable
rock, turd really, called an island, if

this is the case, what is he to make
of the faces he has glimpsed? Not in his
household, not the interminable English
or their wives who never stop scratching,

but those faces out of Africa and from
there, around the Cape of Good Hope—
Heh! Hope! He shrieks, wants to fart
into the wind to demonstrate hope—

Malagas, Malagasy. What is he to make
of the faces of blacks? What is he to make
of the scour marks, not on the skin,
but where places have been dragged out?

And what is he to make of his stomach
each time a black appears in the
distance or irritable wake of some
official? What is he to make of

the itch in his cheeks? He stares
at the mirror and it is unpleasant—
the worst thing—to see this sign
of the secret brotherhood he has entered.

And What of Africa?

The interminable, the foul souring
wind-scarred noise drove him, at
times, against the walls of his house
but he would not let *them* see or
that would go into the diaries too.

He stood at the window, yesterday
was it? and snarled in the direction
of the ocean, its elusive edges
that held him as surely as iron
clamped deer for a game keeper.

In this whole sphere, to be
so far from everywhere, even the
barbarous unknown coasts he had never
hankered after — that sweltering
coast that pulsed off the eastern way

and delivered people more trapped
than he and whom he only glimpsed
or smelt when the front door opened
or a visitor sneezed and complained
about people near animals never named.

He wondered how it would have been,
to be delivered to that coast of theirs
instead of this lump of leaden salt.
He suspected a different reception. Perhaps
he should have left Europe to the fools.

Emperor of Africa. Why had he not pushed
south from the sphinx? Ah. Yes. Entering
that room of flesh-eating stone in the
great pyramid, standing there as the
torches snaked black smoke into the ceiling.

Perhaps if he had not entered that room.
Perhaps if he had not stood alone out of
a whim. Perhaps if he had not inhaled. The
smoke, curling, collecting before his eyes.
They all wanted to know why he ran from there.

Africa. Why had he not, at least, pushed
west into the hot-sand, home
of that worthy general? Hannibal,
like him, making the singular mistake
of falling in love with Europe.

And all the time — he stared east
from the garden as his ears ached
in the wind — that heavy continent
had rested in the protection
of his stupidity.

Another Strange Night

Last night it rose and leered at him.
The face of the island rose, the black
gray rock shining a green light. Not a
man's face. Not a man's. A

woman's face that turned dark,
the colour of a fruit a Portuguese
had sent up in a basket—and
why was a mystery. The

colour of bark. Not a tree
he is overly familiar with. One he has
seen. A deep, deep brown, given a
purple hue. The closest brown comes to

black. And perhaps that skin was
black—he has been studying the
blacks of this island, surreptitiously,
and he has seen how different their

colour is and can therefore say
with some certainty, the colour
was a black which shifted to
a particular sheen, like

the purple of this fruit sent
by a Portuguese just out of
China, or India, by way of
Malagasy and some other port.

He dreamt that this island rose
and peered with a black woman's face.
Her fine white hair. Her top lip
stitched as if once split by a fist.

He dreamt of this face and
now it is with him. It watches
him, hovers even at his bath.
He does not know if he is used to

her. Perhaps she is the island. Perhaps
she is a demon waiting for him to
show the slightest sign of terror. Perhaps
she is his own mother veiled by grief.

Perhaps . . . He touches his face. He
touches his face, tries to remember if
he has eaten any of that strange
fruit of a dark woman's skin.

For the Arrival of a Serious Enemy

Suppose there is only heat
and the stunned hibiscus
leaning against the wall. Suppose
there is only salt rising over
the lawn from the white,
white sand. It crusts, the
air-thinned salt, around the
glass. And in the glass a
lemon-saturated drink not
to cool the mouth, but to
remind the head of heat, to
make a repetition of introductions.

Suppose there is a woman
who stands in the reek of
heat, nursing her arms against
her stomach. Suppose there is
only her and the wall, the
grass and salt rising, from
the white, the very white sand.
And that stunned crimson.
Suppose she loosens her arms
as if she is loosening her
blouse, not to cool her breasts
but to make love to the heat.

Suppose you could name any
flower that snaps itself on
now, in all the garden, coming
out of the spider-haunted greens,
those sweltering greens that hold their
cool centers. Suppose you held their
names on a page or in your
mouth as if they belonged
to your own historic gardens.
Just suppose this is so—bougainvillea,

allemandes, orchids whose wings remind
you of nuns' wimples or other things.

Just suppose your trophy is
a line of palms or a mat
of petals that burn against your
green lawn—and you circle that
burning place like a pilgrim in
search of a greater trial, a
prize in itself. Suppose you
give way to an intimacy between
the roots of your hair and the
embodying heat. Suppose this.
Does that woman come
with the heat and petals

or does she open her big mouth
not to greet or sing, but to curse
in the scalding heat of a
language you do not know?
Does her mouth seer the
ground? Do her eyes rake
the garden into so many
mounds of leaves and things?
Can you see her as she grows?
Can you see her roots seeking
downward, not for water
but fire and a far greater heat?

Gold

The land is rich in gold; if the people were
covetous, a great quantity could be obtained;
but they are so lazy in seeking it, or rather
covet it so little, that one of these Negroes
must be very hungry before he will dig for it.
(17th-century Portuguese explorer)

So, let us talk of quantities,
of measurements and weights
that could tip, yes, the whole
of Europe if one black king sits.

Let us talk of hands covered, as if
with a powder, as if with the tribute
of women's lips which are enough
to make one's eyes water.

Let us be certain that this is
all true and that these kings of
lions, hyenas, tigers and wild men
have no value for the valuable.

Let us know this and see it is so.
If a man is hungry, he will, surely,
sit down and eat what he has pulled
from the black, the very black,
deep and terrible soil.

And tell me, have you noticed how
limitless the strength of these
people is? How their thighs are
not unlike the thighs of the deer
which abound in these parts?

Have you noticed, too, how strong the
women are? How white their teeth, how

high their foreheads? They are, I believe,
the more ferocious of the breed and
pretend, I have noticed, an unfortunate
and disagreeable disdain.

But know this, India will be pleased.
So too the great sleeping land of silk
and all of Europe will glint
from first light to last and even then
burn under the candle's stroke.

Of Prestor John, I report, no sign,
but still the stories come
and such is the tone of the men who
bear them that I know them to be true
and continue to pray for a meeting.

Sunday School

Tell me that old story, the one about
the girl in the schoolyard. The Coloured
girl who was surrounded by boys whose
hair glinted in the late Sunday sun
as if still fresh from a good preaching?

And were they Coloured boys or white
when they found her? I can't remember.
Or were they just men, there in the
late schoolyard where she ran, men
with their bodies erect and driven

to the point of no return, so hard
they broke glass as they passed. And
when they had finished they had one
last joke with a Coke bottle, or was
it a broken broom handle? Do you

remember that story? It has been
running between my legs like blood
for years. My legs are brown. I
keep them covered. I think of her
and how it must have been, giving

birth to broken things—the top
of a bottle or a well-handled broom
long after the men had gone, softly,
back to their mothers and sisters,
wives and daughters. Their stories

of Coloured girls' bodies that
fizz like new Coke, go flat as
piss and taste the same.

The Sleeper

If the grass is yellow and strong
with another sweetness, if the road
dusts itself down after a cold frost-
driven night, if there is a black
bird hanging from an overhead wire
by a saw-toothed wing, if there is
one fence that runs as far as you,
if the air is damp in your lungs
and in your nostrils and hangs
around your mouth in small vapours,
if the skin on your shoulders stays
tight and sharp with subcutaneous
tremors, well, you know this is
no dream but another walk in the
old country you can't call home.

Blow the Wind Southerly

Yesterday—was it?—light rose
like a pale blue train dragging
from the head of a woman
who must have passed
in the high dark. Some

thought, a new wave breaking
so far from any land, running
like a seam the length of the
Atlantic, or the water's many tongues
licking at the moon; some

thought, a whale breaking the surface,
cruising parallel with us,
the ocean washing from her flank
to our barnacled hull and back in
an exchange of delight.

No doubt other things broke
in other imaginations. These are
the ways we discover, out here
a thousand miles from there and
further still from home. Some

have lost "home"—in the first time
        they stumbled on deck and

                were snatched

                        by the moon
Nothing
        prepares you
        for the cool explorations

as that settling silver seeps in
to the softest tissue, takes hold.

49

And. Look how the ocean
lies. Look how it rolls,
exposes every side, heaves up

and opens. Sometimes
a sigh that washes against the
hull and sets a dreamer deep
in its dank air on a course
for dreams that plough and dive

till his body strains and shudders
like a vessel stuck on a reef, spilling
cargo into the indifferent waters
of an ocean that keeps itself delicious;
in daylight, sighing for the moon.

And Bring Him to Me

Yesterday—was it?—light rose

    like a pale blue train dragging.

        He thought, a new wave breaking.

He thought, a whale breaking the surface.

    No doubt other things broke

        lost "home" the first time

he stumbled on deck and was snatched

    while that settling silver seeped in

        and opened something

till his body strained and shuddered

    like a vessel struck on a reef, spilling

        from the head of a woman

who must have passed

    in the high dark

        some thought

Courtship

This man. Visits when he is not
asked. He smiles and his smile
reeks of the highveldt in August, that
sugar smell of burnt grass, soot-
blackened trees. Also that air,
the kind that melts away from its
crusts of morning sleet. It is
impossible to hear anything but
that fire-dried winter ground
as he walks across the stoop
or over the dining-room floor.
I don't trust him, mamma, but
he makes his hands gentle as
they close around things. Every-
thing becomes a baby's head in his
hands and he stands so straight,
like a Voortrekker shielding his
eyes against a northern sun
and when he inhales you'd think
he stood at those first great
Drakensberg feet as if he were
David come, not to slay, but to
make a brother of Goliath; as if
he had arrived to hold God to The
Covenant. This is how
it is, with him. This
uninvited man. Who talks
of a "weird and terrible freedom"
and says he offers me
his life, as a story.

Fire on Board

The water's face today, still as a canvas
after a first wash. The sun clashing
against itself like a Greek beating his
high chest at the walls of an enemy.

One man, unlike, talking about home.
The others are careful not to take
on board the picture he paints, eyes darting.
They know the dangers of thinning blood.

They feel beneath their feet the heat
of the cabin boy's fever now into its
third day. Already they are thinking
of the splash he will make. The talking

man is talking to hide, they know. Praying
men cannot avoid watching their hands
for any signs. Men whose throats have not
held a hymn for decades rake the sky

for relief. Every man feels the heat
seep into his liver and blames the
sour smell rising from his plate,
trades promises for rain or wind

anything that will take the heat
off his body. It clings like scum.
Perhaps they are dead already. Perhaps this
is the way, this waiting in the

scalding cup until the scales tip.
Perhaps this is how it is done,
sweating the truth of a man's life out.
And the truth not in one man's quantity,

but how it mixes—a good mix and that
soldering shield dissolves in a cool
haven of water sweet as a land-left son's
smile in a mother's arms.

A bad mix and . . . hell could not be
worse than this . . . blaming tropic.
And it is wrong to say it is not like
a storm. It is a storm that

raises no alarms, descends like a
boulder, dense, a wall. It
fumes silently, this incalescence,
sets a Bengal drummer below the blood,

and a man would drink a jug of the
keenest lime, call it dulcet
just before his head is clamped
into its final wild dream

in which there is no sanctuary, not
even as he remembers a boy spilling
out into the new snow, falling
open-mouthed into its secret green.

Man in a Room

Darkly, darkly, lying darkly
against the blue sheet, a
man feels the walls of his room
frame themselves around him
like the oiled-green fronds
of a dream he has left
a while ago, or was it
long ago on the other side
of his youth, when he
had the dazzling legs of a
runner and she was his
only wish in her lemon
cotton with those perfect
small dots of white.

He lies against his blue bed
lost in the here and then, far
away from the morning that glows
like a white beach in the eye
of a boy perched in the
crows nest, the phosphorous-rung
crows nest of a heavy man's dreams.

Will he find her? Will he
find the edge of her upper lip
as it ridges under his tongue?
Will he know which way the storm
will blow and how he should
stand when it breaks
against his face, his pallid
fruit-soft face with its
lost blue eyes? Or will she
be the one who reaches up
and turns on the light?

What the Girl Who Was a Cabin Boy
Heard or Said—Which Is Not Clear

We are the finished. We are the people
at the railing, peering into the water,
waiting for the Great White Whale, waiting
for the shark of many jaws. We are the
jokers who laugh like fire falling into
water. We are dulling in our illness and
we are not even going to make an art of it.
We have decided. We have arrived at this
berth and we have decided. We are waiting
for the handkerchief, the sheet, the towel
to cover our eyes. We are waiting to be in a
privacy so inviolate that fictions are
raised to converse with us, that shadows
are read and deciphered to fill the
clever, the final, invincible silence.

Geography Lesson

"What are the four furthest points
of this great continent?"
The Cape of Good Hope, Reverend Mother,
Cape Guarda-foo-ee, Cape Verrrde and . . .
Pushing out into the unexperienced
middle sea, the sea of blue
and Hollywood dreams come through
long-dead stars, Brylcreamed hair,
who sang women into the fullness
of their undergarments. Cape . . .
of The Lost Name, pushing
right up from the spine
of the continent. One point
running clean through to the other.
You could stretch a man into it
like that man in the circles,
stretch a man between the Cape of
Good Hope and the blue sea of
forgetfulness. Or a girl. Put
a girl into the cone of a plane
and send her to yet another
continent of Capes and more water.
And why can't you just walk
across an ocean. Bon. Cape Bon?

"Name the largest river in . . ."
The Nile, Reverend Mother.
The Conga, Reverend Mother.
The . . . The . . . river
that flows from my grandmother
through my mother, into
me and my sister and now
the great-grandson where it waits.

"What climate . . . here?"
Natal-China type, Reverend Mother.

Sister, Miss. Mrs. Lush subtropical
vegetation that breaths out of the— "What is
the annual average . . . ?"—mountains
and over the Indian Ocean, and is inhaled
by the land again, a jealous land— "The
highest mean temperature?"—that measures
its sweat each night, counts its drops like children.

"Who was the first to . . . ?"
Vasco de Gama. Bartholomew Diaz.
Gray-faced men facing out into the
salt, their faces eaten each living
second by the wind; their heads
rest points for gulls and children's
careless attention on school tours.
Men laid out across continents and
oceans, measuring the world into
scales in a trader's warehouse.

And ". . . the founder of this great . . . ?"
van Riebeeck. Jan. Son of Monica
of the Coat. "Coast, girl, *coast*." A woman
the colour of plum wine pooled
into the glistening bowl
of a slim-necked jar. Were there gulls
in her hair? Her eyes, white as
the noise of the beaches her son left
for the Cape of Good Hope where he
stubbed his first blunt toe into blonde sand.
Monica of the night-shade, vanishing
into the white-washed storage rooms
of the new nation's portrait galleries.
Or was she his wife?
"Pay attention!"

On Hearing of the Exiled Prophet *

I heard: out on your island
a madman walked between the dull years
of his sentence for preaching in tongues.
I am asking, is this true? Was he your
father because I tell you I hear him
muttering his next sermons in the long
shafts of my bones? Give me rice
in the shape of your name or something
he will understand, something that will
buy him off and send him on his way
to his high God instead of resting
his fierce chin in my side.

And if he is no relation, speak to him
on my behalf. Ask him, how is it he
has no manners? Tell him, I am your
granddaughter and you are fiercer
than he. Tell him I have another
high god whose arrivals and departures
have more storms and earthquakes than
his. Tell him I am your granddaughter
and you are fiercer than he. Tell him
you have taught me from your well and
I know how to drink. Tell him I will
spill him all over the rocks of his
prison and will not listen to his cries.

If he is a sick old man, longing for his
own lost home, tell him I am your granddaughter
and you have taught me well. Tell him I am
obedient. Tell him you have taught me how wide
my back must be. Tell him I have eyes that see
where the mountains lay against each other like

---

* Dinizulu—nephew of Zulu King, Dingaan—exiled to St. Helena

ngwenyama at the height of the day, the she-
leopard pausing under the fever tree, just
as I look, and her cub bumbles out of the
long grass and tangles in her legs. Tell him
I see this where the river bank goes white with sand
like a half-moon. Tell him this, it is what he needs.

In the Hull

Learning how to dance
this new dance, how
to sway and groan.
Learning how to sing
in a new voice, how
to hold a note deep
and rough in the
deep down there
of my throat and the
deep down there is
where I keep my heart
now, since my heart
was put out to sea.
Learning how to dance
and sing as if the sun
won't come up
if I don't.

Under the Feet of Angels

You do not see them.

        The colour of bones
        after a long time in the sun.

      These faces.

The bottoms of their feet
are deeper than night and they
live overhead in a world that
is never still. It reeks of the
insides of stomachs, bowels. They
shit on us and we shit back in fear.

When All Else Fails

And now, be kind
stars, gods, be kind
whatever names you go by
in our many prayers
and thanksgivings
                be kind
when our fingers break
against the wood that
holds us
                be kind
when we hear our voices
fall flat out of the
childhood we lose
                be kind
in the darkness,
                be kind
when they wash us
heavily and feed us
with rough concessions
                be kind
to our yesterdays, our
back theres, the generations
we shed as we squat
in place among strangers.

To our hands, be kind,
to our ankles, our eyes
                be kind
to our memories
                        even
our forgetting.

Felony

*An Inquest was held at Rupert's Valley, before Thomas B.
Knipe, Esquire, H. M. Coroner, on Tuesday last, 3rd
inst. upon the body of a Liberated African woman, who
had, the night previous, hung herself to the tree in Rupert's
Valley. The Jury returned a verdict of* Felo-de-se.
(The St. Helena Gazette, March 7, 1846)

"*Imprehendedora!*"

Last night, that moon spilled a little
on my mother's hands as she laid
new logs for the fire. My father
whisked the late fly from his face.

    Or was it the owl's wings bearing down,
    was it the spider in the corner of the stone house?

Last night, ghosts fell to the ground
and devoured the path from dark
to light.

A spider pulling stone together makes
more noise than a spirit leaving a body.

Last night, I was singing but
the logs stayed cold.

Dying with those who are already dead
in the house made of gray stones.

Last night I heard my father
drumming the last song
and the moon fell.

The spider spinning its web goes carefully
around the moon caught swinging in a tree.

Contagion

You may think I have come
here to abandon love. You

may think I have come
only as flotsam left idly

on a tide line as love
turned and dragged its skirts

away, as if dragging a higher
moon. You may think these

things. Smell abandonment in
my armpits, obsolescence on my

breath. You may mutter about
sadness or swat at my shadow

to clear the air when you think
I don't see. You may secure your

mouth, your nose with potions that
reek or dip into your secret

cache of lemons and oranges
picked up from port-side markets

along the way. You may do these
things while I curse in saliva

and learn to send my brimming
shadow where once I sent—pah!—kisses.

The Enlightenment Sees Its Face in a Different Light

Why? Why? Not in what comes out
of the hold. Not in that breakage
of strange sounds that mean nothing

and will never be allowed to mean
anything if the whip can help it,
if the salt can help it, but

in the way their voices rise
on the first days—not that
they know, quite, when is day

and when is night, down there.
It's in the way their voices
settle in a rigid silence

that threatens the deck, makes
men's bare feet sting as if cut
on the swabbing command.

It's in the way they moan with that
first swell that tells the middle passage
has begun—a strange thing, that moan

since how do they know down there? They
make that moan, like a ship must,
wrecked far out from salvation

and slipping over into the deepest
trench. They make a sound from their
stomachs, as if they are falling over the edge

of the world, and it takes a civilized man
to keep his hair straight as his course, his
mind fast in his knowledge that the usual things

do not apply to them—their mouths make
impossible sounds until that telling swell
puts an end to why, and the plaguing curve is

lost from their throats and eyes—if you look in
with a light—hold that light high—if you stop to see
when the lid is dragged inside—and it's back to

the business of fighting for a space
to fart and crap, to sweat and howl, those
sounds that grow into the hull's own song.

Even When They Smile They Smoulder

The language of thirst has a way
of drying sweat, of converging
on the thickest word for
heaviness and heat and anger.

The language of thirst blasts
the eyes free from the world of
green things and delightful forms,
even the most loved or most hated.

The language of thirst is for
ravers and the lonely, the
sick and fevered who bring their
fevers to the boil.

The language of thirst bursts
from below, the niceties go,
skin is scalded off even faces
that know how to behave.

Sometimes the Surface of Water,
Sometimes a Mirror—the Horror

It tries a leaf, makes a
mouth and takes the edge
of the leaf, the flat of the leaf

into itself and even then
there is no green message.
It makes a hand and grinds
a stone into its raw palm

and nothing will come out,
nothing will say, nothing
opens and nothing shows

but it wants to know in its pallor
and softness as it waits in the absence
of all that it asks for, those tiny pink answers.

Nightwatch

How? How? At night, or in the high
silver point of noon, there is
moving among us a strangeness

it howls how? how? and we do
not know, no we do not know
as we are, caught in the still

point of our voyage and we
are no longer afraid, we are
no longer men or women, we

are here like souls waiting
while our histories decide
if the strangeness that howls

between us is devil or angel
or if the moiling ball is
the eye of a planet or

a god which has lost itself
or us, or is it one,
or all of us, crying

how? how?

A Dictionary of Survival

Learn very quickly that O is for Obedience—
begin by disobeying your lungs that want something
other than this air, your hands for wanting
clean water, your heart that explodes with each
groan or name that is called out across the dark.

Keep C clean of the hiss that uncoils deep
in the reach of your eyes when the face of a ghost
peers down and covers its nose and you know—
as suddenly as everyone else—the
nightmare will not stop now or forever.

And understand that C is for cutting
as they will say of those ties they call
the temptation we must resist when
we turn our heads in the direction of long ago.

And remember that C is a house for cattle
who were men and women in the eyes of
their parents. And the C of cattle must not be
confused when it is the C of Christ who smiles
at us all. Remember R growls twice in remembrance—

once for forward and again at the gate across backward,
and D is for devils who keep P for punishment
under their fingernails for special days. And S is for
Salvation that doesn't arrive though we learn to pray
for arrival even as we learn to C for crouch
in the long N for a night that will not be still.

Memorial

*M. Souza is the great chief of the slave trade at Wydah. His
dinners are equal to the feasts of Balthazar, and served with
the extreme of luxury.*

Then cast a last crumb in this direction,
cast the curling peel of your half-eaten orange,
cast the left-overs of your legs of lamb and your
platters heavy with the tongues of a thousand
shrikes whose songs go dull in the cavern of your belly.

Cast, cast the bone of a wing which has perished
time and again as you strip it free of flesh — and
did you know the earth is measured by the spread
of wings, turns in the slipstream of the tiniest wing —
cast bones still covered with the trace of your saliva

and the words you utter to a woman who has learned
to keep her mind empty in your presence and her eyes
searching the ground for a memory that does not scald.
Cast the volume of a leaf brushed with rose water
so that I too may keep the stench back and remember

a time before night became this eternal shame of public
evacuation down here, under the floor of heaven. Cast,
chief of traders, one dreg from your flask, one drop of
the palm oil you value so poorly, cast your refuse, your
cast-offs, your cast aways, your dross and discard, your wake

and we will make a feast under your feet, squeeze
all that is left in the most offending offal, the most
rejected morsel. Cast yourself now and we will tally your
fat against our lean because we are not who you think
we are. That woman is our mother, our sister, our beloved.

Floating

He floats, face down
out of nowhere, perhaps
a sailor, perhaps a passenger
bound for a different soil, perhaps
a slave lifted quickly out of the hold
before he contaminated the rest in one way
or another—as if there is anything more
contaminating than being lost
over the rim of the world
in the company of ghosts.

Floating in the skin of the sea.
Arms wide. A sailor,
dizzy over the side of his new ship,
might think, ah
a strange large bird flying
on its back in the face of a blue-green sky
no landlocked man has ever seen and
this sky and bird must be why no woman
can hold a man long enough.

From where does he surface? Floating
so fine and calm. You will learn
there is no name. No face.
Only this, a floating out of the green nowhere
that makes you gasp for breath
like an asthmatic trying to wake
enough, sit up into the dark to keep life in
its place when all it wants, like a tide,
is to ship out over the edge and
splash into the place of gills.

Middle Passage

Nothing moves. Nothing passes.
Not a bird, not a wave. That
bird has been there. That wave,
fluid as resin. The day hangs
flat. It will not pass.
Like disaster.

In a red shirt, a man leaps —
unused to this. He does not even
hit the surface. Only a reflection,
an entered red. Now it is there.
Smoke rises straight into the sky
where he stood and where he stands.

Nothing moves. All disturbance
breaks the mirror and the mirror
grows. We are silent, like ideas
left behind in a silent church.
Nothing passes, not even yesterday's
bright moon.

She Feels the Vanishing Sickness
Move behind Her Navel

I have looked for the blue surface, the pale blue
and glimpsed it only in the sinews,
or darkly, like a family of veins
beneath a tongue as it rose to click and
clack against some action, something
I'd done, back there on that other continent
and now I read the underside of my own tongue
in the cheap mirror in my yellow bathroom.
I read it to see if that is the place
where speech is loaded and catapulted
from. I pluck that purpled blue
like the strings of a taut guitar
that makes this life other than a thing
spread all hidy-ho on a blunt page
by a pristine eye for a neat clean line.
I live in wariness, even if in expectation
of those bold incisions, those neat
clean lines that draw a life.

The Face of the Deep

Sometimes, the water meanders past
our bow and it is we who are still,
unmoving, as if we have become a rock
in the stillness of our own journeys,
stale now as old potato broth the
cook has tried to disguise for another
sour week under the soldering sun.
At these times I feel another
face of water moving under
a dark deep wind, here,
here in my chest. Oh,
will no-one reach in
and save me from the
inland sea that
rolls and sways
and opens,
to cover
me?

Eclipse

Today, today. A black sun.
I heard the beating of wings
like blood in my ears when
a voice cried out — bird lost,
supplicant in tears. That sun's
single foot striding its
metallic length across that
blackened field of dreams.
Men known to spit at laughter
shortened their necks — turtles
hauled on the deck of a quick
fisherman. Men who
carried no memories doubled over.
I tasted salt at the silver
table. I saw the great silver-
backed, shark-tipped ocean open
and those men and women — yes
there were children too — opened
their eyes and their lips were
silver with waiting. They opened
their mouths and the beating
of wings drummed at our bodies.
I heard them. I heard them.
Their voices rose like branches, the
branches of trees left behind. Their
voices were leaves on the branches
of trees left behind. Their voices
dripped from the branches like
water over our heads and my
heart was a land thirsting for
water. This is what I heard.

Adrift

Tonight I start something. Stop.
I stutter like light seen through
palms on an island that lays
in the deep distance of a
night we slip through. I
start to see a channel of
dark currents whose silence
enters our hull and soaks
up into our feet, our heads.
You, oh you. Can you see
how silent my head has
become, how silence covers my
face like a visor? I am on
a vessel of silence. All sound
is illusion, reflections against
the dark water. And islands
slipping by are reminders of
what is forever unknown.

In the Maw

Perhaps it is not that I am
dreaming of, but praying for
oblivion. Perhaps there is an
escape I have not considered, a
voyage I have not heard about.
Perhaps this creaking from
week to week, slow, dumb
year to year, is the journey
I have yet to consider. Perhaps.

Then. Why? Why? Living where
the only burning river is
slow anger. Living where the ocean
is thick with ghosts from old,
old wars and older lies that
are the only things with any
life left in them. It's them
you catch when you cast
your line. It's them that
bite and, bitten, you have
no choice but to reel them
in and make your meal.
Yes. Perhaps it is this which
makes me dream—a spinal poison
I tell you exists. It exists
in mouths that open daily
and are closed hard on soft
words. The softer the flesh
the harder they close. Perhaps
it is this which makes me
look up, for meteors, for
an announcing single letter,
an ice-held branch
of lightning. Perhaps it is the
snake swallowing into my
throat, muscle-band by

muscle-band, that makes it
hard to breath, hard to stop
worrying about delicate tissue.
I tell you, I feel its downward
journey. I feel its homeward
yearning. Nothing will stop it,
trick it up. Nothing will recall
it. Cinnamon. Lemon. Orange peel.
I've made offerings of sweet
lettuce, tried burning frankincense
sandalwood and vetiver. I've carried
all the right stones—amethyst, rose
quartz, hematite, even held lapis marbles
in the palm of my hand while I
slept. I've rubbed rosemary on the
soles of my feet and cedar wood into
my navel. I've opened my mouth as an
invitation to the sun to fall straight
to my throat. I have sought deliverance.
I have tithed and measured out obedience
without stinting—to no avail. Perhaps
I will die choking. Perhaps this is how
we all go, crushed from the inside like
ice and swallowed by silence.

In The Wake

Days, weeks passed, and under easy sail,
the ivory Pequod had slowly swept across
four several cruising-grounds; that off
the Azores; off the Cape de Verdes; on the Plate
(so called), being off the mouth of the Rio
de la Plate; and the Carrol Ground, an unstaked
watery locality, southerly from St. Helena.

Breathing at night when breathing is hard,
when the chest rusts and squeezes
against the lungs. And the lungs filled
with spume caught in the narrow passages,
thickening like egg white. God,
for a dry place. High and dry. Grass that
crunches under the heel and cuts sheeps' tongues.

But it's the lost sea that breaches white
against the walls of night without warning
and when it comes, breaking across the bow
of the bed, troubling the shelves of all
my books, the sea that rises turns and all
those voices, their coral bones, the pearls
that were their eyes, look for an on-shore wind.

One voice. One. Oh one voice. Doesn't it sing
anymore? Is that it, flagging behind the years
that fashion themselves out of nowhere, like
walls of vapour that rise out of the sea. A place.
Find the place that years come from
and the veil will lift and seas will settle
back where they belong, islands grind against the
sea as islands, no more. No more sea-fey. No more.

Out there, unstaked, my own tongue. Such
thirst. Such thirst. Like a long night in the
dark heat of December or January—a southern

December or January, hear. Years of days, weeks
under the uneasy sails, navigating the channels
that push further and further away from the taste
of a single word to call my own. Oh, my mouth —

a river without sweetness, only the dry
scuff of landed men walking, pegging miles
not even for themselves. If I say yes to that
sea wind again, if I open the black O of my
mouth and show its stinging stub, if I swallow
the sea and the face of the moon, will there be
will there will there be a . . . a . . .

"Sod you!" One side of the sail was wet.
His cry broke off.
No-one looked up. "No-one?"
"Moon-fey." They lay down dreaming —
hot sand turning into the women —
the smell of the sea, of sperm falling —
dissolving in the astringent sea.

Now the storm-blast's come and god it's strong,
you can feel it chasing out. Up north it's south,
from here its there so you go through mist or snow.
But the sad bald thing is there's no strange bird
to split the wall of things. The things are here,
the things are there, I tell you they're all around.
Time's space is a shroud packed with everything

from the smallest stone to me. I'll be a good ship,
I'll love the waves, I'll take the deepest trough,
but I want, I want, just one sweet word
for one sweet taste that doesn't taste of lies,
or dead men's sweat or dead men's salt
from the pearls that were their eyes.
I'll sing through things, make dead seas change
into something rich and strange,
de-da, de-da, de-da, de-da, de-da-de-da-da-hghhgh.*

---

* to be read as sound of breath

ii.

Days, weeks, the open-ended trough
breaking the edge off the land like
bread. In the waves that fall from
daylight to dusk out here, searching
for an unstaked locality south of years.

Way over there. I saw the spout of a dream
break against the edge of the land like
a ghost in its infinite loss. Asking for
a shape, asking for a way to touch each
to each. The slow sweep of years already.

I have asked my mother, she does not know.
Out there, out there, a ship rolling like
a wagon over the sea—bring the loss home
safely to me. And in the clearing yard
under the stichwork of gulls, not knowing.

The thing is. All this time. Rinsing a mouth
out there, out there with the new deliveries
that taste like pineapples to the investors,
I begin to taste the edge of a new salt and
I tell you, my hair turns white with shock.

A dancer, the water's single edge. Gone, gone
so quickly it is long ago and the memory
feeds like an unstaked love feeds itself
into your marrow or under your fingernails.
I turn my face to each wind, waiting, tasting.

It is in my cells. This hull keeps upright, but
so quickly from long ago a million memories
roll like a sea wagon, creaking under the
stitching cries of birds I have never seen
but who bump against the backs of my eyes.

God, the light rolling against itself
breaking out there so quickly, the edge of the island.
Did you see it? I swear. I swear, like some

native taught the agonies of a new language, the
island broke through for a second. Do you believe? Me,
a woman with birds stabbing the backs of her salt-sharp eyes.

An Easter Confession, of Sorts

Oh, God. Another night I was full of it,
I accused the sky of being empty of seraphims
and having not one drop of excess light.
And I refused the rising moon one scrap
of admiration, one favourable glance.

I was glad of blasphemy, pronounced it
on quick lips and my mouth crushed
the immaculate syllables of belief, even hope.
I promised coffins and dreamless sleep, headlessness,
a gutted heart and highways of blood
which silly men would read from aeroplanes
to declare they'd found the signs of gods. I believed
in stones, only stones and incisions,
dead and dying rain, catastrophes
the prophets would not have faced
even in their holiest beards and gowns.

I poured nothing where libations were
common. I stamped on new leaves and
I spoke of perversion in the prayer stalls.
I am let loose. I am riding on my true and
bronzed talons. I am among you even as you
sit and I am the hell your scriptures
have yet to calibrate. So, speak to me
and tell me why I must hold your faces dear,
as if they are the faces of lost angels, light itself.

For Strength in the Face of a Powerful Enemy

At times. Beauty, only beauty
moves beneath my skin, a traveling
thing that will not rest but burrows
for a home. Not here. Not here, it
nudges. This place, this collection
of cells around the knuckle, around
the nipples, the half moons of her
nails have already been named and
will not hold another. In her head
there is no room and in her heart
there is no place strong enough
to take the impact.

Let me travel then, in the shadow
of beauty, carrying its shadow
where it burrows, under my skin.
Let me hear its whispers and let
me survive.

Desire

Who was it that stopped at night,
made the window hold its cool, clear
breath under the slowing summer air?
Who slipped through the room, celebrant
of the free hours, dancing into the
government of shadows—the night—
and turning my shoes over to see
where I had been all day, and by
which routes I had arrived and
departed? Who read my palms as they
lay open on the blue sheet? Who
traced for the frailest history
and measured my life line and found
both short and broken? Who breathed
onto my face? Who left me like this,
seized by a waking knowledge which is
that bereavement some call longing?

Devilry

I am accustomed to my shadow's disobedience.
It lingers, twists its determined neck towards the edge
of the continent in that northerly direction
where fog fowls language and will not allow my southerly
invitation, my antipodean promises through.

Some days it is as if I am a dream of hers
but my shadow is undisturbed by its
tenuous hold on my heels. Yes, some days
I can hear her move from room to room
in her northerly abode, dreaming.

And I am looking for a book of spells
for the dreamed. I am looking for the
spell that will turn a dreamer's head
to see the shape and form of the hand
she sometimes holds, makes sad with desire.

Aubade

When silver first looks over its shoulder
    and the cool meridians of her arms begin to
fall away, when at last the sweet all-night
    weight shifts from your chest, your belly and
you hear the men cough below,
    reach for their last quids of twist,
why, oh why this dream of voyaging
    under the rosary of stars told softly by lovers,
as islands made of tiny shells,
    the pink spines of cuttle fish, slip away?
No. You refuse, rage even, against
    the growing light—nothing short of the planet
turning—while the moon-loving water dulls
    and sets its copper kettle down for those
who cough and reach for themselves.
    Their relief as their bodies stamp on deck. They
search the horizon for any sign that will
    feed old dreams of coconut milk and parrot fire
deep in the hips of women who gleam
    dark as the hull of a ship and warm as yellow sand.
And while they inhale you will not let them
    see you, covered as you still are, by silver and
holding within those signs that tell,
    "I am her whore, her harbour from which she collects
each night her fingerprints, I hold them
    as jealously as men hold yellow sand beneath themselves
and when they rise, arrive in the breakfasting
    hour, happy to be fresh out of darkness, hearing the
rough tobacco of the first mate's voice,
    I hoard my silver and secret cache and will not be
amazed by talk of the horizon looped with islands or
    steeped in palm wine, since I am in mourning as I wait,
waiting to see if she will find me again
    when she is done leaving her fingerprints in
other moonstruck harbours that find themselves
    made lawless as water with many pearl-seeking tongues."

For a Lover Who Keeps to Another Hemisphere

At night is my frailest hour, my
lands end, when the smoke of old
fires has dissolved and lies lightly
in ash that shifts at the slightest
sound. At night, you know how it is,
how all my poems are silenced by
even the walls when you peel loose
from the darkness and lower this
ladder, my body, into its cold bath of
solitude.

Sweeter and Dearer

Like a seam the length of the
Atlantic, or the water's many tongues
        the ocean washing from her flank
to our barnacled hull and back in
        the ways we discover, out here
a thousand miles from there and
        by the moon as no woman can grab
in even her hottest moment. Nothing.
        And oh. Look how the ocean
lies. Look how it rolls. To
        our hull. And sets a dreamer deep
in its dank air on a course —
        cargo into the indifferent waters
of an ocean that keeps itself delicious
        like a pale blue train dragging
from the head of a woman
        who passed in the high dark.

Is It Not Sweet?

In the high dark—some
　　licking at the moon, some
　　　　exchange of delight,
　　further still from home, some
　　　　preparation for the cool explorations.
Exposure at every side. Heaving up
　　for dreams of ploughing and diving
　　　　in daylight, sighing for the moon
　　in the dark head of a woman
　　　　who must have passed by.

Southerly, Southerly

Out here
So far from any land
the flanks of a wave breaking
over the hottest moment
the hull ploughing and diving
as only a woman
who keeps herself delicious
for the moon can

Moon

O
>barque
>>bearing
>my
lover
>to me
>>in the
>water's
many tongues
>the seams
>>of the
>softest tissue
>>have run
>the length
of this
>body   in
>>preparation
>its cells
compress
>like sand

Now That She Is a Woman Herself

Sometimes, before anyone else has dragged back
from that relentless sleep of the weary,
she lies listening,
not to the light hissing
through curtains—so white
they are blue—not that alone,
but to that ceaseless circling
between even the most extreme continents
of her head as it weighs
against the pillow. And her head weighs
as if it will never be light enough
to lift without tearing tendons.
And she wishes, thinking
of a simple glass of water
on a white heat day,
for laughter like a frond of green.

With the Art of Birds

She sings. And unclean mouths break open
their unsuitable language, clean the backs
of their teeth to make a new place for
saying her name. She sings. And what is
good is victorious, and I see red carnations
of desire float over the water. I see the lily
whiten and throw its pollen out in a small
dome of yellow welcome for the procession
I want to make, the one that should mark
the preparation of her instep as it arches
over the cool tiles and makes an avenue
of abutting molecules all the way to
my blue bed. And can you hear how
still it has gone, how even the walls
will not breathe or allow any thought but of her?

She Observes the Blue Bird

Now, still, oh still, still day
poised and just poised in the stall
like a bird above the desert, holding
this—the red throat of a flower that
holds itself to a vine, so still, so still
you do not notice how still while
birds peel from tree to tree in search
of hemispheres under the same emerging
moon. The bluest day dips and pauses,
goes still, oh still as the eye of
the bluest bird on the stillest branch.

A Riddle to Save Face

So, to dream in the eerie light
of one's solitude, lay honey from
the front gate—only the front, mind—
to the foot of one's blue bed
is to invite hungry things in the
inarticulate hours. And that, in
the face of the monstrous desire to
love and be loved, is a tale of
dragons and other nonsense.
But have you seen the sea
mirror all the hours of the day
and sink into its own face at night
when the jealous sky is off elsewhere?

The Cabin Girl Sees on All Sides
Evidence of the Dream

You know the thread holds, she
said. It holds across distances
like these we've laid, tracks
only the gods can read. And out here
the white flags are not of surrender,
but welcome, and light makes
mirrors of walls, of water, your
neighbours' eyes as they dream
of other things while you keep
your senses honed for any landing.
And be sure to have your hands
unclasped, she said, making
fish leap as if yearning to give up
their many-circled scales.

She Looks Up and Points

Now, she said, you have never seen
skies like these, and the west sank to its
sepulchral knees, and the east dusted its
night sails while the birds drew their dividing
lines like spiders taking the thread of
each breeze from tree to tree till they'd
steadied the ground and stitched us together
with their quick, sharp beaks and pearling
eyes. Now, she said, you will never see
skies like these anywhere or ever again,
and the day closed round on itself, slowly,
to the sound of her prayers, her terrible
prayers that burn even water.

The Beautiful Flood

One night, she said, the ocean
rose, laid trees on their sides,
took lives and claimed roads.
I heard her saying this.

I heard her breath, as she
paused and the sound
of her breathing as she lay was
the sound when night blows sleep away,
and the upright are laid low
and life is claimed
all along the wave breaks
of even minor catastrophes.

One night the ocean came
claiming marvels — the blind
boy's left hand which drew
perfect wings on his mother's walls,
the tongueless girl's box of stones
which sang out at lies stitched
into the hems of very important men.

She said this, her elbow making
the bed dip near my head. And the
moon opened its smooth mouth
and swallowed sleep as she counted
the claims levied that night. I
heard her counting in fabulous numbers
that cleaned up after themselves
and left no stench, or bloated forms
though lives were claimed
all along the wave breaks.

What Is Out There?

What do they mean, swimming up
like that, out of other sounds?
The scent of apples left in
the pantry months ago.

The room that spins. My head.
Rain that blew in. The bricks
that open. The way the
room tilts. This. is. not.

fair. Without looking, there are
pores in my skin. And. Listen,
is there no pity? Is there no end
to the grating? The powdering?

Some of the Women

Some of the women knew how to fold their hands.
Some of the women knew how to stand at their gates.
Some of them knew the size of a man, the length of
his promises, the value of his smiles long before
he reached their gates. Some of them listened anyhow
smiled back and learnt to punch dough first thing
in the morning or last thing at night.

Some of the women kept their knees together,
their gates closed. They liked being landlocked, never driven
by the sea. They kept their curtains moving, and the tips
of their tongues sharp. Some of them weren't driven to
madness, some of them didn't go dry. Some of them sang
Bread of Heaven and baked it just as good and some
of them found each other like honey-driven birds.

Behind My Back

Sometimes, you know, I am looking back
at the women mad with themselves, standing,
their hands deep in the week's dirt—their
own and not their own—their voices rising
like question marks or a believer's incense,
the steam from their own cooking,
in search of a song caught from someone
else's lips or straight from their own
longings; always longings, I think, looking
back. I look at them winding their hands
deep into the water. The soap. The clothes
wrung and wet like entrails a sangoma could read.

Sometimes I hear them and they are still
calling, but the things they say are gone.
Only the madness, the solid, daily morning
till night madness that made them sing, hangs
over me, before me and I listen, watch, as
hard as if I want to catch it, that madness,
be like them—gone so deep now they are wells—
or like the contents of their wash buckets
because, surely, this is what is happening.
Already I listen to them and my insides
wash themselves free of the years of dust
that cling to me, separate me from them.

She Confesses

This water grazes the beach,
roughs up the years of tiny
molluscs whose lives reappear
in the rustle of each incoming
wave. And the ghosts of those
lost at sea push their mouths
to the vents of crab holes,
sucking the air so newly washed.
And I am afraid. I am
afraid of lying there too,
sealed away, serving a scavenger's
imagination and crabbed art
that chases white sails on those
lateral grids, hungry for the
new land, the pristine place
that always must be named.
Oh mamma, I fear an illness
has set in again—not one
you can cure. Yes, immune—
it is—to your potato creeper
that drew the puss from my
leg. This lays me in my yellow
bath and I can't hold on
to the sides. They groan and
lurch and walls fall away
to reveal oceans and places
I have never been to in this
weak, sea-troubled body. I
am speaking to you, mamma,
I am telling you this—I am
a liar. I am afraid of all
water. I have never made a
single voyage except in the
hands of orderly timetables and
indifferent agents. There has never been
abandon. Sea spray makes a deep

shudder. I am afraid
of all water that drains away.
And where does it go when it
turns and pushes through evening
or daybreak, or the highest noon,
or the coolest midnight?
Where does it go when it has
swirled over your feet, or
when it has survived each
detonation on strong days?
It is not enough to learn those
early lessons that surf
onto blackboards in a teacher's
careful arcing arrows—blue for
the rising air, green for its descent
and a poor brown filling a land
I could not identify. It
is not enough to know nothing is lost.
I have lost my good body, mamma.
The one you kept in health. I
am in my yellow bath, waiting.
Will you be there when I drain
away? I think it will be
like nothing I have known
and I confess to not knowing how
to behave, or what to feel.

Land Ahead

On all these sides, the ocean's blue
face, its green, and on laden days the
slate gray that draws short-lived
squalls out of the distance—on all
sides there is a green hungering for
steady ground, for grains of sand,
not salt. And it is time to leave
this tilting land, this windstruck life.
It is time to open the doors of houses,
not hatches on cargoes brought from
the mouths of half-understood words.
It is time to stop the lurching ways,
the sea-born ways. Time.

Headwind

Crouching under the raw wind, under the
trader's wind—it carries the messages of continents
to other continents, of trees to the planes, of
the haloed head of a ripe plant at the foot of
a rock on the east side of that, yes that, hill—
crouching under the weight of a wish to be
elsewhere, to speak freely, each word, each
letter, the vowels that love the intricacies of
a mouth, the great moment of a throat's opening—
always, always on the name of a god—perhaps
a god that has never been named, but slips
something of itself into your mouth in order to
be free of its terrible, its all-in-one self—and to
feel the soft, the tender coil of an inner ear, perhaps
hers as she receives my message of love. Ah. And
then that turning point, that corner in her
where it all happens, where it all turns and
that traveling, that word-drunk truant, splashing
into my ear will know how dire, how frail and
vacant it is to be all of nothing.

Then. On other days, there is only . . . nothing
but the shapes of things, nothing but the
sound of my own voice, my top lip, my
bottom lip, my writing, sending
messages into the single dimension, the
starting and . . . Is it the final point? The
"as well"? Such lies. That haloed head
opening from its pores, a feast for the
wind, the plains, the crook where two
journeying mounds of soil meet short of
merging but make a vacant place for
filling, for taking root, for crouching
into one tight vessel that waits for just
the right moment and just the right opening.

The Cabin Girl Sings, of Love, Reluctantly
and into an Empty Sky

Sometimes the deck is a point in a
large and revolving sky and I swear
all things are in it, even the smallest
button I once lost on the way home
from some place I have already forgotten.

Sometimes it is I who am on the deck
lurching in the concatenation of
winds that hurl around a cape and,
oh, the millions of directions it
all flies in, but always there is
this, slowly steady with one
eye on the large and revolving sky.

Sometimes it is that the deck is
a point in the sky and someone is
watching the quiet old dance people
make across a wooden floor they have
laid and polished themselves in the
shadow of lives that lie behind them,
the lives that lie ahead.

Sometimes the point is the sky
streaked with the trajectories of
thoughts someone scans and frowns
at to see, to find, to hear. And
it seems this has been the whole
of her life and when the sky peels
away, drops and glides on a smooth
wind she asks the bird, "Do you
have a message for me?"

And When I Write the Muscles in My Chest Move as if in Flight

Sometimes the eye of the bird
is a sky that is moving
among the molecules and over
twenty different landscapes
someone has crossed, even lived in,
perhaps longing for the soil of at least
one to wear in her pinions in those
high-necked altitudes that see
the endless couplings of man and
woman and woman and man and
man and woman like a garland
circling the broken globe.

The Voyage Out

Clouds on the western horizon—
we took them for islands, began
smiling and allowed our throats
to open. But they were only
clouds on the western horizon.

A pipe dropped, rolling on the deck—
we looked for the bird chucking
deep in its woody throat, thought
of trees, their shade across our bodies, not
a pipe dropped, rolling on the deck.

Moving from stern to bow, a breeze—
we sniffed land-fed food, gave ourselves
full mouths and heavy stomachs and
felt our feet dancing on true ground, not
moving from stern to bow, a breeze.

Late, so late and across the line
that cuts the geographer's world in halves
we slipped into the southern sky like
a cloud fooled by a bird's blue wing so
late, so late and across the line.

Into the second half and closing
all distance, opening another, we gave up
hope of adventure, of calling mountains
by our names, for our lives were slipping
into the second half and closing.

St. Helena — Time Line

15° 55′ south latitude; 5° 49′ west longitude
within the limit of the South-East Trade Wind
400 leagues from the West Coast of Africa
10.5 miles long, 6.25 miles wide
28 miles in circumference
30,300 acres of surface

*The island, when observed at sea, presents to the eye the appearance of
an abrupt and rugged rock, divested of tree, shrub, or herbage. A nearer
approach brings in view the central eminences, distinguished by a softer
outline, clothed with verdure, and towering to the clouds. Advancing still
nearer, the scene again changes and the green summits are shut from
sight by the intervening craggy and stupendous cliffs, that seem to
overhang the sea. The great elevation excites in the mind of a stranger an
idea of being too near the land* . . . (Brooke, *A History of the Island
of St. Helena, from its Discovery by the Portuguese to the Year 1806*)

1487   Bartholomew de Diaz rounds Cape of Good Hope.

1502?   21st May. Admiral da Nova Castella arrives at an island which
        he names St. Helena.[1] The island is "inhabited only by sea-
        fowl . . . and it is supposed that this was the first time its
        shore had ever been visited by human footstep."[2] The island
        is used as a watering stop, its location kept secret from the
        rest of Europe.

1516   Dom Fernão Lopez jumps ship at St. Helena. He and other
        Portuguese sided with a failed Moslem attempt to end
        colonization of Goa in 1512. General Alfonso D'Albuquerque
        (the "Caesar of the East") ordered that the traitors have "their

---

[1] Philip Gosse, *St. Helena, 1502–1938* (London: Cassell, 1938), 3.

[2] T. H. Brooke, *A History of the Island of St. Helena, from its Discovery by the Portuguese
to the Year 1806; to which is added an Appendix* (Clarendon: Harper Collins, 1808),
35–36.

right hands, the thumbs of their left hands, and their ears and noses . . . cut off." Lopez also had his hair and beard scraped out with clam shells, a practice known as "the scaling of the fish" (Gosse, 4–5). Gosse, Blackburn, and others write that he was left alone on St. Helena, Brooke that he had slaves. He is left biscuits, some dried beef and fish, salt, fire, old clothes, and a letter telling him to show himself to passing ships so that they can know if he is alive or not.

1526   Lopez is taken to Portugal, walks to Rome, returns to St. Helena.

1545   Lopez presumed dead.

before   "Two kaffirs [*sic*] from Mozambique and a Javanese man and
1557   two women slaves swam ashore from a ship. . . . They soon multiplied to twenty. . . . For a long while the blacks defied all attempts to capture or destroy them. . . ." (Gosse, 11; he gives no reference for this).

1557   Bermudz, Christian Patriarch of Abyssinia, lands at St. Helena, "away from the disorders of the world." His slaves escape. He "despairs" of "human help" in old age, returns to Portugal (Gosse, 12, quoting from *The Portuguese Expedition to Abyssinia in 1541–1543* [Hakluyt Society, 1902]).

1588   Thomas Cavendish of the *Desire* seizes St. Helena. He describes a "marvellous sweet and pleasant" place filled with lemon, orange, and pomegranate trees, date palms, parsley, sorrel, basil, fennel, annis seed, mustard seed, radishes, and other herbs. There are partridges, pheasants, Guinea cocks, and thousands of goats. A note is made of three slaves, one of whom comes from Java.

1652   16 April. Dutch settle Cape of Good Hope and take slaves from Madagascar, Bali, Sri Lanka. Cape Governor Jan van Riebeek enquires about taking slaves from St. Helena.

1658   English East India Company establishes a colony at St. Helena.

1792   British Government orders end of "importing" slaves at St. Helena.

1815   17 October. Napoleon arrives on the H. M. S. *Northumberland* to begin his exile. He comes ashore at 7:30 PM to avoid the crowd's stares. The crowd brings lanterns. He meets thirteen-year-old Betsy Balcome. Governor Hudson Lowe refuses him the title of Emperor, insists on calling him General as well as by the Corsican version of his name, Buonoparte, instead of the French Bonapart. Napoleon says he last heard of General Bonapart in Egypt. He is set up in Longwood. His party includes the Marquis de Las Casas, Baron General Gourgaud, the Counts Bertrand and Montholon, the doctor O'Meara and valets. Most of his retinue keep diaries. Even Betsy is mindful of her place in history. At forty-two she will publish a book of her *Recollections of the Emperor Napoleon during the first three years* . . .

1821   May 5th. Napoleon dies.

1833   Emancipation decree at Cape of Good Hope. Effective 1838.

1835   Ordinance 1 — *An act for the Abolition of Slavery.*

1838   *Act for the Abolition of Slavery throughout the British Colonies.*

1865   Slavery ends in America.

1890–97   Zulu chief Dinizulu, son of Cetawayo, exiled to St. Helena.

1898?   7 April. Margaret Delphine Ritch born at Jamestown, St. Helena. Her father is said to have been a first or second generation freed slave. Nothing is known of her mother except that she too was born on St. Helena. Margaret Delphine has three sisters and one brother, perhaps two. Her father works for a man called Lord Albu. Margaret Delphine's mother dies sometime before 1910, the date when her father remarries a girl aged sixteen. The family leaves for Southern Africa as part of the Albu's household. Her father, or brother, poses for a photograph in his full regalia as a member of the Ancient Order of Forresters.

1910?   Margaret Delphine works as a kitchen maid on Albu's farm, located at what will become the Conservative Party area of Benoni in present-day Gauteng. She swims in what will later be called Benoni Lake and reserved for "Whites Only." Her daughter later tells, "She used to swim with the water snakes. They used to come right up and swim around her." Sometime after 1910 her father leaves for Bechuanaland (now Botswana). Her sister Agnes is born there.

1920   Margaret (known by now to the family as "Finnie") meets William Bennett (Bill) Blandford. They marry in Cape Town. The marriage certificate, whose same hand signs their names for them, signs her as being born in the Cape. She objects, but the document is official, it stands.

1933ff   Finnie and Bill are in Johannesburg. By now they have two children, Veronica (Sally) and Vernon.

1948   The Nationalist Party wins South African election. The first major Apartheid legislation is passed: The Group Areas Act. Finnie and Bill now live with their children in Hondsebek (Dog's Mouth, the end of Doornfontein in which coal and other mining money lives and which Hondsebek services).

1954   Verwoed, National Party Education Minister, has written the Bantu Education Act to "teach non-whites" how to "best serve their betters." 4 August. Sally has daughter, Yvette, in the corrugated tin room in the backyard of a house in Van Beek Street where she, Finnie, and Bill live. Doornfontein has been swallowed by the Dog's Mouth and is years from its heyday. Yvette's birth certificate reads "12th December." Family secrets.

1956   18 November. Sally and Owen Christiansë have daughter, Lynette, at 27 Curry Street, on the corner of Van Beek Street. Finnie and the midwife, Sister Strydom, deliver Lynette. Finnie comes out of the bedroom and says to Yvette, "This is your sister." Two old people from St. Helena are there, they come every year at this time. Yvette never remembers their names.

1959   Yvette is sent to the white, Catholic, Belgravia Convent near Jeppe with a faked birth certificate and a lecture from Finnie not to confuse it with who she really is: a Doornfontein girl, a Coloured girl. Yvette goes to school with two faces.

1964   Sally moves herself and her daughters to Cape Town. Finnie and Bill begin grieving. The girls go back for school holidays, but Doornfontein has shrunk and the house on the corner is full of dogs and cats, and an old-fashioned radio that still wants to glow in the dark before it warms up and gives forth. Finnie talks about her mother and sisters, her brother's disappearance, her stepmother, St. Helena. And Lorenço Marques and the people who come from there.

1967   Sally moves to a suburb next to Doornfontein. The girls go to St. Angela's Ursuline Convent. Finnie has Alzheimer's, talks of Lorenço Marques, her mother, and the sea around "the island." She goes to Baragwanath hospital with pneumonia. The granddaughters are terrified when they visit because (a) she has shrunk and weeps on their hands when she sees them, and (b) they know they can never pretend to be anything other than Doornfontein girls, Coloured girls, standing there in that ward of over fifty black women, many of whom smile, and offer sweets and conversation. Finnie's mind clears and she introduces the girls. She sits up and is proud, but her body remains tiny. Yvette swallows many times.

1969   Sally moves herself and her daughters to Swaziland to "escape the madness of the Republic." Finnie grieves. Sally decides to move her parents, too. In Swaziland, Finnie talks constantly about the island, her mother, and the sea around the island. Bill cannot cross the border for more than a month without losing his pension. He dies in Johannesburg. Finnie attends his funeral and doesn't know why.

1973   December. Sally migrates to Sydney, Australia, with her daughters.

1974   June. Finnie arrives in her "new" country. At the beach she thinks she is in Lorenço Marques, talks about her mother, her sisters, getting on a boat to go the island and visit. Her granddaughters think she is mad. In July Lynette gives birth to a son, Jean-Pierre. Finnie thinks her great-grandson is Yvette. She begins knitting for the baby. She dies a month later.

1993   Finnie bumps against the back of Yvette's head. Yvette begins writing: "My grandmother's island is wrapped . . ."

*Yvette Christiansë is Assistant Professor
in the Department of English at Fordham University.*

✦

Library of Congress Cataloging-in-Publication Data
Christiansë, Yvette.
Castaway / Yvette Christiansë.
p. cm.
ISBN 0-8223-2386-9 (cloth : alk. paper).
— ISBN 0-8223-2421-0 (pbk. : alk. paper)
1. Saint Helena Poetry.
2. Women, Black—Saint Helena Poetry.
3. Slave trade—Saint Helena—History Poetry.
I. Title.
PS3553.H7286C37   1999
811'.54—dc21   99-25490   CIP